My Faith in Broccoli

Essays on Racism, Privilege

& Food Deserts

Kay Bolden

Dedication

To all the children of Warren-Sharpe
Community Center
past, present and future.

Contents

Acknowledgements

My thanks to:

The board, staff, volunteers, youth and families of Warren-Sharpe Community Center

Jayme Cain, Publisher, Joliet Times Weekly

Medium Publications

P.S. I Love You (Dan Moore)

Creative Conduct (Regg Nash)

Other Voices (Teri Jo Walker)

Crossing Genres (Allan Rae)

Chapter 1

Magic Beans

There were fourteen 3-year-olds in the preschool class at Warren-Sharpe Community Center. About half came to school every morning with a bag of hot chips and a can a grape soda passing as breakfast.

"We serve a nice, hot breakfast every morning," I'd remind the young moms and dads, trying to discourage this habit.

They would smile politely and ignore me. Their kids wouldn't eat our breakfasts, and no one knew it better than I did. They wouldn't eat scrambled eggs or yogurt or oatmeal. It was sugary loops or powered donuts or nothing.

The battle would continue at lunch, when mashed potatoes were grudgingly accepted, but carrots and green beans and tomatoes all hit the trash. "Yuck" was the word I heard most often, right after "Mine!" and "No!"

At our weekly parent meetings, parents would urge us to serve the children hot dogs or chicken nuggets, French fries or pudding cups. But we continued to resist. Just like we resisted turning on the TV and spending too much time in the computer lab.

Getting this video game generation outside to play was just as exhausting as getting them to eat real food. It was too hot, or too cold. It was boring. Why can't we watch a movie? The grass itches. The slide is too small or the monkey bars are too high.

Our aging playground was serviceable — even if we did have to rake the sand once a week for drug needles or beer bottles or used condoms — and the vacant lot was perfect for playing kickball, when the city remembered to mow. We made do.

One night, we invited a guest speaker to our parent group to talk about nutrition. She told us we were living in a "food desert" and started explaining its technical definition. A few parents looked at me in confusion.

"It means," I interrupted, "that you can walk around this neighborhood and buy all the heroin you want, but you can't buy a head of lettuce."

A soft voice in the back of the room asked a simple question.

"Why not?"

Why isn't there any food in this poor, black neighborhood? Why are there fast food joints and overpriced gas station markets and church soup kitchens, but no grocery stores? No farmer's markets? No real food?

Why not?

Why can I step out the front door and flag down a drug dealer in 5 minutes, but I need three hours and two busses to get to a grocery store?

The meeting ended shortly thereafter, but the thought didn't go away.

Why not?

Why don't the people who live here have access to real food?

Like a grain of sand trapped in an oyster, the question began to burn and writhe.

Why the hell not?

On my way home, I counted eight vacant lots around the community center. Lots that were formerly homes and families. Wasted space that was now filled with weeds or litter or abandoned cars.

Eight of them in a 4-block stretch. We only needed one — and not even all of that. Just a few square yards to plant something.

But what?

"They don't eat beans," the preschool teacher reminded me. I hadn't forgotten. But they didn't eat anything, so we might as well start with something easy. And considering I'd once killed a virtually indestructible aloe plant, easy was crucial.

We planted pole beans. One plump seed per child. We scraped away the weeds and dumped some potting soil from the dollar store on the hard, grey soil and made some holes. (Our lessons about soil contamination were far in the future.)

Maybe, we thought, if they did the planting and the watering … maybe if they watched the beans grow … maybe if we read them bean stories and practiced writing "B" in the dirt with our fingers and dreamed up bean recipes … maybe they'd at least taste something green.

Looking back, it wasn't much of a plan.

Until those little magic beans started to grow.

"Can we go outside and check on our beans?"

"Will it grow all the way up to the sky, like in the story about Jack?"

"Look! Mine is the biggest!"

Soon the older kids in after-school program and summer camp were out in the garden as well. We needed their big-kid muscles; there was no water faucet outside, so they formed a bucket brigade every day to water the plants.

Over the next two years, the garden spread like wildfire. We badgered the city into donating 3 more vacant lots.

We designed one just for education, where we taught history by studying the food traditions of other cultures. In our Victory Garden, we planted turnips and cabbages and beets, and learned about European immigrants.

In our Three Sisters Ridge, we planted corn and squash and beans together, like the Native Peoples of Illinois.

In our Huck Patch, we feasted on collard greens and okra and yams, and we studied slavery and civil rights.

Our Cocina Mexicana taught us lessons about our Mexican neighbors to go along with the tomatillos and cilantro. Even our herb garden gave us intriguing ideas about natural healing.

On the other lots, we grew vegetables. Broccoli and tomatoes and 8 kinds of lettuce, and peas and peppers and melons.

We had no idea what we were doing. What needed full sun? What needed shade? Why are the leaves yellow?

Who planted the onions upside down?

Still, like magic, everything kept growing.

We sent the kids outside to pick salad for their own lunches. We sent veggies home with them. We invited curious neighbors over to help us weed — and eat.

The local newspaper took notice of this little garden in a high-crime, low-income neighborhood and ran a story.

Our city councilman came for lunch, then the mayor, then a United States Congressman.

We wanted the kids to stop eating hot chips and grape soda for breakfast. And for the people who lived around the center to have some real food. So we planted some beans in a vacant lot.

They turned out to be magic beans.

Turned out — like magic — we were able to unplug our kids from their video games and get their bodies in the sun and their hands in the soil.

Turned out — like magic — while we were arguing about whose turn it was to water the cucumbers, and whether the tomatoes had blossom rot, and if the squirrels ate the corn — we were learning some other stuff too.

Yes, we were learning about the environment and plant life cycles and soil temperatures.

U.S. Representative Bill Foster, IL-11, joins the kids for lunch in the garden.

But we were also learning how to argue without name-calling.

How to resolve our conflicts with our words, instead of our fists. Or our guns.

How to respect other people's space, other people's feelings, other people's contributions, no matter how small.

We were learning that we could create something new with our own hands.

We were learning how to grow community.

While the kids are planting collards and squash and peppers, they're also planting the seeds of change. They're cultivating new ways of thinking, nurturing new ideas about how their lives — and their community — can be someday.

Then, unbelievably, First Lady Michelle Obama invited the children to the White House to tour her Kitchen Garden.

August 17, 2015 at the White House

And while it was a spectacular experience for them to shake hands with the mayor and to visit the White House, none of that compares to what happens regularly now in our parent meetings:

"Can you tell me please, what is Swiss Chard? And exactly how do I cook it?"

"We made zucchini bread with the squashes Matt brought home last week."

"I've got too many tomatoes! Somebody trade me some jalapenos?"

And what happens regularly now in our lunch room:

"Can I have some more salad, please?"

Akeeli Lindsey has gotten over her fear of spinach.

One of the fifth graders wrote a thank you letter to Michelle Obama which said, "I really like your garden. But ours is a lot bigger than yours. We have a lot more people to feed I guess."

I guess we do. Growing food and sharing food can change the world.

The garden provides food to 40+ families during the growing season and was named an Obama Legacy Initiative Site. This story first appeared in ThriveGlobal.com on October 17, 2017.

Chapter 2

In Our Own Backyard

In Our Own Backyard was a column in the Joliet Times Weekly, covering environmental justice and climate change, and their impact on black families in food deserts and low-income neighborhoods.

Originally published April 13, 2017

When the Trump administration took office on January 20, 2017, environmental advocates took aim. The Peoples Climate Movement (as well as other groups) has pushed back against White House efforts to dismantle the Environmental Protection Agency and is working to build a grassroots coalition that links climate change with racial and economic justice.

Since taking office, the president has scaled back or eliminated professional staff positions in the EPA; filled the agency with climate change deniers; and issued executive orders rolling back environmental protections on clean air and water. The appointment of former Oklahoma attorney general Scott Pruitt to head the department is the most telling; Mr. Pruitt spent most of his career battling the EPA's regulations, and he personally believes the agency should be stripped of its authority. [Update: Scott Pruitt resigned as chief of the EPA on July 5, 2018, amid numerous scandals and allegations of misuse of millions in taxpayer funds.]

What does this mean for our families and our neighborhoods?

It means we are at risk.

It means we can no longer ignore threats to our environment, and tell ourselves that it doesn't affect us, or that there's nothing we can do about it anyway.

Here's why:

Low-income communities and communities of color are disproportionately impacted by environmental crises. We are the first ones hit and the last ones informed when our soil or water is contaminated, or when pesticides or manufacturing waste in our neighborhoods have breached safety levels. We often feel both politically and economically powerless to demand answers or to take action. According to Kari Fulton of the advocacy group Empower DC, "A rollback on environmental regulations hits our communities first and worst."

We have to eat. Our ability to grow food is dependent on clean soil, clean water and clean air. Access to healthy food is not just a matter of nutrition – it's a matter of human rights.

We can't keep our children healthy with chemically altered food, water from toxic pipes, and letting them play in polluted lots. In fact, if we don't demand clean food, clean water and clean air, we can look forward to increases in public health crises at all levels, from asthma to cancer.

Gretchen Dahlkemper, National Field Director for Moms Clean Air Force, says the destruction of the Clean Power Plan and EPA regulations "will harm real lives and impose an incalculable cost on our healthy, our economy and our moral leadership in the world."

Note: The People's Climate Movement mobilized for a national March for Climate, Jobs and Justice on April 29, 2017 to demand environmental protections for our communities.

Chapter 3

Rise Up!

Originally published May 3, 2017 in Joliet Times Weekly

Among the estimated 200,000 people who participated in the People's Climate March on Saturday, April 29 in Washington, D.C. were thousands of teens and young adults. They came by train, by car and by the busload from every state; their voices were loud and their message was clear in their chant: The Oceans are Rising ... and So are We!

Young people convened the day before the march to talk about the role of youth in the climate movement, to build art installations and banners, to hear from inspiring speakers and to build relationships with other youth from around the world.

Mark Hoyt, a college student from New Mexico, participated in a drumming ceremony called One Earth, One Heartbeat, One People. "It was nothing like I've ever seen before," he said. "So many of us coming together for the same purpose." He vowed to go back home after the march and get more involved with environmental issues in his hometown.

The Youth Gathering was only one of dozens of pre-march events, which included sacred water ceremonies by Medicine Women from Indigenous Peoples, workers' forums, worship and potlucks at various churches, poetry slams, leadership training, poster making parties, teach-ins, panel discussions on building a green economy, and LGBTQ rallies.

"We're all in this together," said one marcher. "And we better start acting like it."

The climate movement is sometimes criticized for not being racially diverse enough, especially since low-income communities and communities of color are often hit first and hit worst in environmental crises.

But the People's Climate Movement, which describes itself as "a broad-based coalition of environmental, immigrant, youth, indigenous, Latino, racial justice, economic justice, and faith-based groups and labor unions demanding an economy and a government that works for working people and the planet", went to great lengths to address and include environmental racism in the march and rallies.

Mary Kay Henry, International President of the Service Employees International Union (SEIU) which supported and participated in the march, said, "As working people, people of color and immigrants, we're here because our families are disproportionately hardest hit by pollution and climate change's impacts. Every day SEIU members and our communities see the impact of toxic pollution in our air and water. We march because we are on the frontlines."

The next day, Paul Getsos, National Coordinator of the People's Climate Movement, responded to news reports that Congress has reached a compromise regarding a continuing resolution (CR) to fund the U.S. government until September. "Congress took a solid first step in rejecting the Trump administration's proposed budget cuts to the EPA by proposing to fund it virtually at current levels until September. However, this Congress needs to continue to stand up to an administration that favors corporate profits over clean air and water and places our workers, communities and our people at great risk."

Protesters in DC and sister marches across the country and around the world urged government leaders to act on climate while creating family-sustaining jobs, investing in frontline and indigenous communities and protecting workers as the nation transitions to a clean and renewable energy economy.

"We know it's going to take a lot of work," said Alexis Brown, a high school student from New York. "But that's why we have to start now."

Chapter 4

A Funny Thing Happened on the Way to the Climate March

Originally published June 14, 2018 on Medium.com

I got busted.

Four lanky teenagers, 2 boys and 2 girls, watched me approach the check-in table at one of the many Youth Convening events at the People's Climate March in Washington, DC. I mean, I knew I couldn't meet the "youth" criteria, but hey—I can identify Kendrick Lamar in a lineup, can't I? I was rockin' my #RiseUp t-shirt; I'd left my Birkenstocks at the hotel; and my backpack was suitably ripped and dirty. Maybe my youth is long gone, but surely, I could fake it enough to hang with the cool kids. Right?

Right???

The girl with curly hair sent me a big smile and started toward me, with the other teens straggling after her.

"Hi, are you looking for the Elder gathering?" she asked brightly.

No. I'm absolutely not going to anything entitled "Elder".

Big Blond Nerdy Dude wanted to know, "Do you need a hand with your pack?"

This pack I've carried—fully loaded—on rocky trails and mountain paths all over the world?

Uh, no. But thanks.

Finally: "How can we help you, ma'am?"

And there it is. I'm a ma'am.

Busted.

I almost cried. And I must've looked upset, because they hastened to assure me I was welcome with the youth groups, even if I, uh, didn't exactly, uh …

"Oh, just come on in!" Curly Hair grasped my elbow and swept me into the gathering. I sat on the floor in the back, like I used to do as a kid in the 1960's, while my parents and their friends made speeches and burst into righteous chanting without warning.

Kids scooted over and made room for me. They passed me flyers and water bottles and Starburst. Some thoughtful person dropped a few condoms on my lap. I sang and clapped and wept and sang some more.

The day before, I'd spent a few hours in front of the White House with the young Queer ResisDance protestors, and eventually danced down Pennsylvania Avenue with them. (I can only pray that there is no photographic evidence of my dancing.) They gave impassioned speeches about the intersection of human rights and climate change and connected saving the planet to the struggle against homophobia in ways I hadn't considered.

At the march round-up earlier in the day, young people of the First Nations spoke only with their drums. They taught us the pattern and the pulse, and implored each of us to participate, to feel the power of the rhythm. To let our mouths be silent and let only our hearts speak.

I took my own turn at the beating of the drums—but it was not the sacred sound which uplifted me, but the teenagers themselves. Idealistic. Resolved. Determined.

These memories all came rushing back to me after the Marjory Stoneman Douglas High School massacre, and the rise of another wave of student activists, demanding safe schools and common-sense gun legislation.

As a professional youth advocate, I often speak and write about what young people need from parents, teachers and mentors to grow into healthy, curious adults.

But here's the truth: we need them far more than they need us.

We need their drive and their vision and their occasionally snotty attitudes. We need their insight and their single-mindedness.

We need their self-absorption and their kindness to strangers. We need their lack of respect for authority, their refusal to accept reality, and their willingness to fling themselves, headlong, into whatever they love.

We need their techno-brains because God knows the next mutation of the cell phone might actually kill me.

As the Youth Gathering ended and the teens headed off to build art installations or Snapchat themselves into a frenzy, I realized my legs were asleep and my back hurt and all I really wanted was an Uber and a lobster roll and a shot of Jack Daniel's.

"You okay, ma'am?" Curly Hair was back with her entourage. She helped me up off the floor and gave me a hug, granny-style. They'd been at the front of the room, talking passionately about climate change and LGBTQ rights and gluten-free pizza.

The fate of the world is in these young hands. And, for the first time since January 20, 2017, I'm feeling optimistic.

Chapter 5

Both Sides Now

Originally published August 17, 2017 in Joliet Times Weekly

Heather Heyer is dead. Last Saturday in Charlottesville, VA, she was mowed down in cold blood, in broad daylight, on camera, by a white supremacist.

I never met Heather. I don't know if she liked yoga or hockey. I don't know if she was shy or outgoing. I only know that she felt strongly enough about love that she stood up against hate. I only know that she joined the peaceful protest against armed terrorists, to add her voice to the call for justice.

Whatever your political leanings, if you are a human being with a beating heart, you were sick and disgusted at the sight of that car, speeding viciously through the crowd, intent on murder and destruction.

Whatever you think of Southern history and statues of Robert E. Lee, you were horrified at the sight of those men, strapped with guns and ammo, carrying torches in the dark, chanting "Jews Will Not Replace Us" and "Go Back to Africa Niggers".

At least, I hope you were.

There's another group of people – some well-meaning, some not – who perpetuate the myth that "both sides" in this tragedy bear responsibility for the death of this innocent woman.

The president -- who should be a voice of reason, justice and equality no matter what party he represents -- used his platform instead to further this lie of false equivalence. In his latest presser, he went so far as to compare George Washington – the founder of this nation – to Robert E. Lee, who led a war to not only maintain the savagery of slavery in the South, but to destroy the United States itself. To literally rend America in half.

There's a word for what Robert E. Lee did, and the word is treason.

Trump continued to push the untruth that counter-protesters in Charlottesville had incited the attacks against them, that those who were beaten, spat on, shoved and killed were somehow as responsible as the gun-wielding thugs who committed the assaults.

There's a word for what Trump does, too, and the word is mendacity.

The Unite the Right demonstrators came to Charlottesville with guns to protest the removal of Lee's statue, and to uphold all the Confederate flag represents: white supremacy. The counter protesters came – armed only with the Constitution – to uphold the highest ideals of America: equality for all.

And here the myth of "both sides" is laid bare. Equality is not the other side of white supremacy. Equality is middle ground. Equality is consensus and justice. There are no other organizations out marching with guns, insisting on the supremacy of THEIR race or religion, demanding the deportation or outright murder of those who are different.

Only the Nazis and Ku Klux Klan do that.

But when you're accustomed to being superior, I guess equality can feel like oppression.

In the "well-meaning" category are people who say they hate violence and racism but both sides, left and right, need to unite. I thank anyone who is anti-violence, but please let me clarify something for you:

One side is domestic terrorists, wearing swastikas, carrying torches, chanting "Heil Trump" and "Fuck You Faggots". One side ran over a woman with a car, then ridiculed her on their website for being a "useless slut".

When one side is Nazis, committed to the deportation and/or extermination of people of color, there's no path to achieve unity. How do I, a black woman, find unity with those who want me dead? Who reject my very humanity?

When one side is Nazis -- supported and enabled by a president – we don't need to wait and see what they'll do. We know what they do. Ask any veteran of World War II.

When one side is Nazis, you need to be on the other side.

Heather Heyer is dead. On her last Facebook post she wrote this: If you're not outraged, you're not paying attention.

I couldn't agree more.

Chapter 6

Love is a Warrior, Not a Saint

Originally published May 1, 2018 in Other Voices on Medium.com

After the Nazi march in Charlottesville, VA last year, when Heather Heyer was murdered, my inbox and Twitter feed were awash in "love trumps hate" memes, and videos gushing that there's only one race—the human race.

My friends—of all races—sent me stylized Michelle Obama quotes and John Lennon songs and cute puppies playing in the sun. Red, yellow, black and white … we're all so precious in God's sight.

I appreciated their kindness, and their efforts to allay my fears. But I felt uneasy, too. It was unnatural, all this saccharine-soaked love.

My newspaper asked me to write a special column, calling for unity. Calling for hope and peace and kindness.

I had no idea how difficult this small assignment would prove.

Because my words—always so measured, so even-handed, so focused on fairness—abandoned me. For the first time in a long time, my natural inclination was not to soothe, not to make peace, but to incite.

And every story I wrote had the same theme bleeding through.

Rage.

Not just for the white supremacists and their collaborators—although they were first on the list.

No, I was also enraged by every single person offering thoughts and prayers or singing *Ebony and Ivory*. I was furious with everyone waving peace flags and wearing safety pins on their lapels.

I was astonished by the sheer banality of it all. Apparently, we should put our collective fingers in our ears and sing La-La-La at the top of our lungs, in hopes it will drown out the avalanche bearing down on us.

I wanted to line up all the do-gooders and feel-gooders and scream into their faces:

Are you insane? We are under attack! This is not a video game.

I know—wallowing in anxiety isn't helpful. A positive outlook is necessary in challenging times. And ordinarily, I'm hopelessly optimistic. Ordinarily, I'm a glass-half-full kinda girl.

I'm the columnist who wrote a dozen stories about racial unity, urging everyone to find common ground. To do unto others. To be patient and kind.

I'm the black mother who carefully taught her kids to love what Thomas Jefferson *wrote* and still despise what he *did*. To live with their guards up, but still believe in the promise of America. To absorb a million microaggressions and injustices, but still be able to say, unequivocally, I Am Not Your Negro (James Baldwin).

I'm the teacher who put my faith in the poetry of the Constitution. Even though it never meant to include me or mine.

Cue the universally misunderstood Martin Luther King quote:

Hate cannot drive out hate. Only love can do that.

Let's ignore for the moment that King was shot down like a dog. Let's put aside that once **Hate** is in control, you won't be able to **Love** your way out of the concentration camps.

Where did people get this ridiculous notion of love?

Love is not soft or pasty or shimmery or mystical or precious or cottony or dusted with cinnamon.

Love breaks bones.

Love is not sprinkling moonbeams over pipe bombs or blowing kisses to Klansmen.

Love stands ankle-deep in a pool of somebody else's blood or vomit and doesn't flinch.

Love is not harmless or weak or timid.

Love is a warrior, not a saint.

I was forced—by my own words—to admit I was not writing authentically. That I was playing to the crowd and the clicks, instead of heeding my own natural voice.

I left the paper not long after. They were never happy with my work after Charlottesville. I began writing for the Resistance.

And for myself.

Finally.

Chapter 7

Out of School, Out of Food

Originally published May 30, 2017 in Joliet Times Weekly.

An earlier column about the Trump administration's rolling back of Michelle Obama's nutrition guidelines for school lunches – and what it meant for low-income kids -- sparked some thoughtful feedback from readers.

One reader, a parent of a special-needs child, wrote that schools shouldn't be feeding kids at all, and that it's not the job of the school to manage kids' diet and health. "Let's give parents back personal responsibility and trust they can raise their own children and manage their health without government. Like our parents did."

I whole-heartedly agree that parents who can take responsibility should do so; my concern is for families who cannot adequately feed their kids. Additionally, government has always been involved in our food, from subsidizing farms to monitoring for safety to approving pesticides to disbursing tax dollars to school food vendors.

There's no getting the government out of our food system (and if we could, it would create more problems than it solves), so we need to ensure the food coming to our kids is as clean and nutritious as possible.

A local teacher wrote in, saying she agrees that kids should have nutritious lunches, "but I cringe when I see the food students throw away each day." She says the veggies, especially, are often overcooked and unappetizing, and kids won't eat it.

I know first-hand that this is a problem. At Warren-Sharpe Center, it took almost a year to wean the after school and summer camp kids off of fried foods, Kool-Aid and processed cheese.

The tipping point was the garden: when the kids started growing the food, cooking it themselves and serving it to their friends – eating it was a natural result. Over time, their taste buds evolved, and kale chips became as cool as French fries.

But we're working with 40-50 kids at a time – not hundreds or thousands. For teachers who already have a myriad of non-teaching tasks in the course of the day, pushing veggies at lunch is problematic at best.

Another parent writes that every school should have a garden and make growing food part of the daily curriculum. Needless to say, I think this is great solution. There are over 7,000 gardens in schools across the country, where food is grown to improve nutrition and create outdoor science learning.

By the time the average American child is in fifth grade, he/she is consuming up to 34% of daily calories from fast food. It's cheap, easier to find than a farmer's market, and the salt/fat/sugar combination becomes the flavor profile kids are accustomed to.

In the end, there is no substitute for family involvement, for reconnecting our kids to real food, and for demanding viable community resources which support access to healthy fresh food for everyone.

Chapter 8

Vegetables Against Violence

Originally published August 10, 2017 in Joliet Times Weekly

What do you do when you're totally stressed out? Many of us – far too many – use food to soothe ourselves. A relationship break-up? Time for Rocky Road ice cream. Financial pressure? Triple burgers and cheese fries make everything feel better for a few minutes.

What do you do when the stress is continual? When you can't escape your worry?

A recently released Duke University study revealed that teenagers stressed by exposure to bullying and violence do what we do: overeat.

Youth consume more fatty, salty, unhealthy foods and beverages on days they had to deal with violence, either as a victim or a witness, and suffered from fatigue due to poor sleep for several days after.

More than 20 percent of U.S. adolescents are classified as obese. Obesity rates are higher among low-income children, and the rates are highest among Hispanic and African American children ages 12 to 19.

But it's not restricted to communities of color; it's a nationwide trend. According to the United Nations, the United States ranks 28th on global health goals, below many other wealthier nations, due to our high rates of death caused by violence, HIV, alcohol abuse, childhood obesity and suicide.

The United States also lagged among other high-income countries on maternal and child mortality, reflecting large differences in the accessibility and quality of healthcare. (Iceland topped the rankings, followed by Singapore and Sweden.)

Many other factors play into youth obesity, of course: access to healthy food, family genetics, nutrition education, peer pressure and our overall "junk food" lifestyle. But for the first time, there is scientific research backing up the idea that exposure to violence – just seeing it, thinking about it, fearing it, or worrying about it -- affects our teens' physical health in the most basic ways.

Children and youth exposed to constant stress are also more likely to experiment with drugs, engage in risky sexual behavior, and exhibit violent tendencies themselves.

In Lexington, Kentucky, at least one community is trying to tackle both problems – violence and teen obesity – at the same time. Food co-ops in low-income neighborhoods pool their money and buy fresh veggies from local farmers, giving families access to healthy food. The co-op itself provides a safe, community gathering place for young people who feel handcuffed by fear.

In my own backyard, I see the difference in behavior between kids who spend time in the garden and kids who don't. Youth who grow food – for themselves and their neighborhood – learn about more than plant life cycles and nutrition.

They learn to work together cooperatively. They learn to disagree without name-calling, and how to resolve conflicts with their words instead of their fists.

They learn to appreciate the value of being part of a project bigger than themselves.

Chapter 9

What are We Wasting?

Originally published April 26, 2017, Joliet Times Weekly

"Everything is connected to everything else," is often called the First Law of Ecology. But it's often hard to see – or care about -- the connections while we're busy working, raising families, caring for older parents, and dealing with the never-ending tasks and crises in our daily lives.

We have evolved into a disposable, throwaway society. From disposable diapers to one-time use razors, convenience trumps conservation. Why wash dishes when paper plates are cheap and plentiful? Who cares if we left the lights on all night, or if the food scraps went into the trash instead of the compost bin? What's the big deal?

Our disposable lifestyles waste far more than water, electricity and food. We are wasting time to recover and heal our planet, and we're wasting the talent of a generation of children who are growing up in toxic environment.

And while efforts to recycle harmful materials have been rising steadily, there is still a huge gap between suburban and urban communities. Recycling, reusing and reducing in low-income neighborhoods often lags far behind more affluent, educated neighborhoods, for a variety of reasons:

People living with daily economic stress don't perceive recycling as a priority. When you are trying to pay your light bill, or scrape up gas money, it's hard to be concerned about whether your plastic water bottle hits the trash or the recycle bin.

There's no clear pay-off. We don't always see or feel a direct connection between tossing that soda can in the trash, and how toxins from landfills leach into groundwater and soil.

We're not informed about how excessive levels of lead, arsenic and other contaminants can affect brain development in young children, cognitive functions, health problems and behavior issues.

There's a lack of ownership in the community, a sense of powerlessness that winds its way through every aspect of life.

What can we do?

Cultivate plants in our own backyards that help heal the earth. Geraniums, hyacinths and sunflowers soak up heavy metals, and beautify your neighborhood.

Reuse things we don't need. Donate them to nonprofits rather than tossing them. Or band together with neighbors to have a garage sale.

Save money and support our local economy by repairing clothing, shoes and appliances instead adding them to the landfill.

Stop buying disposable items whenever we can. Drink water from a refillable, non-plastic bottle; some have built-in filters.

Switch to reusable grocery and produce bags. Trillions of plastic bags are discarded each year and they can take up to a thousand years to degrade. While they're degrading, they're releasing harmful chemicals into the ocean, groundwater and soil.

Buy pesticide-free produce from local growers, or grow our own. Adding more plants to our diets reduces consumption of meat from commercial farms. Runoff from barnyards, feedlots and cropland carries away manure, fertilizers, ammonia, pesticides, livestock waste, oil, toxins from farm equipment, soil and sediment into our water supply.

When we waste water, energy and food, we also waste money, time and talent. It's a lifestyle we can no longer afford.

Chapter 10

No Food? No Justice

Originally published April 19, 2017, Joliet Times Weekly

With the closing of Certified Warehouse Foods, the food and retail "desert" on southeast side of Joliet is nearly complete. Our community retains dollar stores, liquor stores, overpriced gas and unhealthy fast food – but no economic plan that will actually drive growth and opportunity

Ironically, the lack of food in our neighborhood is not only proof that the current strategies have failed; it can also be the catalyst we need to create change.

What can we do?

Invest and support urban agriculture. Build a local, community-owned food system that reflects and responds to the people it serves. Initiate and reinforce community-led efforts to create a sustainable food system.

Recognize the economic power we already have and spend our dollars wisely. Buy neighborhood-grown produce and support neighborhood-owned businesses.

Grow community leaders as well as food. Reclaim our family traditions of cooking together, eating together and sharing with our neighbors.

Create opportunities for people to get involved, learn new skills and communicate effectively with each other, and with prospective investors.

Become our own agents of change. No one will invest in our

community if we don't do it ourselves first.

In the past, discriminatory practices and policies confined people of color to certain neighborhoods, producing "bubbles" of high-poverty areas. The loss of manufacturing jobs and rising unemployment helped bolster this isolation.

Historically, these areas were also systematically starved of resources and investments communities need to thrive, like financing for homeownership, business investment, public transportation and safe recreation. Families who could afford to leave did so, accelerating disinvestment.

What's happening on the southeast side now is a microcosm of urban distress all over the country: low-wage jobs, lack of investment, crumbling support systems and infrastructure – and a lack of food.

Neighborhoods play a significant role in the development of our children. The availability of good-quality food, access to health care, good schools, reliable child care and after school recreation, exposure to crime and violence – these things shape our children's future, and their ability to thrive in a competitive world.

According to a 2015 study by the Urban Opportunity Agenda, poverty reduction itself has the potential to be an economic engine. Without reducing poverty, economic growth spurts in the overall society will result in an ever-widening gap between the haves and the have-nots.

There is a high price to pay for this gap. We pay in increased health care costs, in prisons, and in declining global influence.

We must commit our ingenuity and our resources to using food as a vehicle for social change. Bringing people together around food – a universal necessity – is a way to build community, and to create lasting social, racial and economic justice.

Chapter 11

The Myth of White Fear

Originally published May 6, 2018 in Crossing Genres on Medium.com

When three professional black women either didn't notice or didn't bother to respond to a white woman waving at them across the street as they left their Airbnb, they found themselves surrounded by 7 squad cars and a helicopter.

A helicopter.

They were detained, subjected to questioning, and called thieves and liars by the cops, one of whom said he'd never heard of Airbnb. Even after showing their booking info and calling the landlord, they were questioned further.

This isn't fear. This is entitlement.

The white neighbor suspected robbery, she said, because of the suitcases. She lives across the street from an Airbnb house, but apparently has never seen people coming or going with suitcases. She noted that "they didn't wave back" when she did.

How dare they.

How dare these black women work hard all year, take a vacation, and not curtsy when a white woman crooks her finger at them.

When two Native American teens arrived late at a college tour, and were too shy to speak to anyone, they were surrounded by campus police and searched. They were so upset after that they immediately got back in their car and drove home to New Mexico.

This isn't fear. This is bone-deep white superiority.

The "nervous" white mom told the cops the boys "wouldn't answer her questions" and "they kept their hands in their pockets".

How dare they.

How dare these young brown men ignore the command of a white woman.

How dare they take a college tour they had booked and confirmed in advance and stand around quietly. Saying nothing.

One officer reportedly told the boys' mother later, "Well, maybe next time they'll speak up when someone asks them a question."

Maybe next time, they'll do as they are told.

Maybe next time, they'll acknowledge the authority of any white person present who demands to know their business.

Philadelphia. Starbucks. Two black men waiting for a friend. Just sitting there, as if they have the same rights as white customers.

Handcuffs. Arrests. Nine hours in lock-up.

This isn't fear. This is backlash.

Like the 2016 election, when the most vicious, brutal and bigoted elements of our society were not only given center stage but applauded and normalized.

This is payback for having to say "Mr. President" to a black man whose intellect, morals and family were above reproach. Who could not be effectively stereotyped as lazy or stupid or sexually aggressive. Whose Ivy League education and soaring oratory made them feel small and lacking—instead of proud to be his fellow American.

How dare he.

This is correcting for the last 8 years by hunting down, murdering and setting ablaze activists who insist that Black Lives Matter.

White people are not afraid. They are emboldened.

They are using law enforcement as their own personal stormtroopers, pointing a finger at any person of color who doesn't show them the deference they're due. It's a longing to return to pre-Civil Rights Mississippi, when we had to control our facial expression and demeanor, not speak unless spoken to, not look a white man in the eyes.

As these situations occur more frequently, it's a message to all of us:

You better not act like you are equal to me.

You better remember you're only safe as long as I say so.

You better stay in your place.

White people are 79% of the police force; 78% of the House of Representatives; 90% of the U.S. Senate; 70% of CEO's; and in control of the vast majority of the nation's wealth.

We are no danger to them.

You know who actually endangers white people? Other white people. 84% of white murder victims are killed by … white killers.

Stop calling it "fear" and call it what it is.

White Supremacy.

Chapter 12

Here Come the Politeness Police

Originally published June 26, 2018 on Medium.com

With the current White House policy of ripping helpless children from their parents' arms and traumatizing them for life—euphemistically called "the border crisis"—I'm seeing the predictable flood of posts, memes and essays exhorting us all to be civil, to respect differing opinions, to be kind to each other.

I saw a similar surge of the Politeness Police after the Nazis murdered Heather Heyer last year.

I understand the impulse to focus on something we can control, like our tone or our attitude, because the reality unfolding around us—the daily, sometimes hourly, reports of callousness, abuse and corruption—is mind-blowing in its vastness and its intensity.

That deep anxiety gives rise to the desire for peace and calm, so the Politeness Police begin to drum things like this again and again:

A difference of opinion does not mean the other person is a bad person. We have to respect each other.

This seems like a perfectly reasonable, sensible thing to say.

Except that it drives the false notion that all opinions are of equal value and deserve equal respect.

Should I "respect" the the opinion of white supremacists, for example, that my black life is not as valuable as theirs? Or the opinion of bigots that my queer son is not entitled to equal treatment under the law?

Is the idea that innocent children should be separated from their parents just another "opinion"?

Views like these, when held by those in power, become national policy and then law. The consequences can be deadly.

Perhaps—if your privilege keeps you safe from the consequences— you might see them as "differences of opinion".

But for people of color, for LGBTQ people, for immigrants, for non-Christians, for any marginalized group— and for any human being with a conscience—this is not a difference of opinion.

This is life and death.

What kind of mental gymnastics are necessary to rail about Robert DeNiro's language while our government is putting toddlers in kennels? How did anyone's priorities get so screwed up?

Do you really expect us to be concerned about speaking nicely while we are under siege?

"If peace means keeping my mouth shut in the midst of injustice and evil, I don't want peace." Dr. Martin Luther King, Jr.

If you truly want peace, then you'll join those fighting for justice.

Two wrongs don't make a right.

This is a common assertion by people who have already seized what they wanted, and now will prevent others from doing the same. Even the current push for civil discourse reveals this vile double standard.

The Politeness Police are conspicuously absent when the current White House occupant calls black NFL players "sons of bitches", or women in the Senate and the House "Pocahontas" or "low-IQ individuals". Or spends 5 years saying the President of the United States is not an American citizen. When he disrespects our democratic allies and praises the bloody acts of dictators.

Just a brief scroll through his daily Twitter feed will provide enough petty insults and character attacks to gag a maggot. There has never been a president, of any party, to descend to the depths of his vulgarity.

On this, though, the Politeness Police remain silent.

There are two sides to every story.

And—finally—something we can all agree on. There are indeed two sides to this story.

There is equality, and there is bigotry.

There is justice, and there is oppression.

There is right, and there is wrong.

I know which side I'm standing on.

And I'm not always so fucking polite about it either.

Chapter 13

Questions & Answers

In response to questions about racism, homophobia and white privilege from readers from January through June, 2018, Medium.com

Question: Do you think that racism is still running rampant?

Answer: Racism has a thousand layers and has had many centuries to grow and spread. Bigots like that caller in 1968, like the KKK marching in Charlottesville last year, like Holocaust denier Art Jones who is running *unopposed* for the GOP nomination in the IL-3 congressional district—they are easy to spot. It is the institutional racism, the internalized beliefs that I find much more insidious.

It's the people who would never burn a cross on my lawn or call me a nigger, but who will defend and rationalize police killings of unarmed black men. It's the people who say "Why does everything have to be about race?"

It's the people who want to define for *people of color* what "real" racism is, or decide what black people should and should not be offended by.

It's the people who reach a level of hysterical rage over football players on their knees, because they *simply cannot accept* that it's about racism, and they must demonize the protesters instead of the perpetrators.

Power concedes nothing without a demand, without struggle (Frederick Douglass). That struggle is uncomfortable, difficult and yes, sometimes violent. People with privilege will fight (with their votes and their financial power and their media outlets and sometimes their guns) to retain that privilege.

We are, as a nation, schizophrenic about race. We are a country built on the genocide of the native people, the enslavement of Africans, and the exploitation of immigrants. Yet we cling to this narrative of equality and justice and freedom … even while the belief in white supremacy is embedded into our very founding documents.

Until we are willing to look those truths in the face and begin the long process of reconciling our ideals with our actions, until we do that, we will be seeing the ugly realities of racism.

Bigots who attack us accomplish the very opposite of their goal — we are not intimidated. We are more resolved.

So., We don't give up. We don't quiet down. We keep fighting the daily fight. We keep telling our stories. And as Martin Luther King said, far more eloquently than I ever could: The arc of the moral universe is long, but it bends toward justice.

Question: Should whites have repercussions for calling the police on blacks for no reason?

Answer: People will not change their behavior until there are significant consequences for their behavior. These behaviors arise from white supremacy, but as a legal matter, I'm not sure how they'd actually prosecute them.

The consequences, in part, must stem from the way we engage the police, and how the police respond. In Philly [the Starbucks incident], for example — the responding officers should have been able assess that situation and resolve it. Given police violence against black men in particular, I found myself just being grateful they weren't shot.

How sick is that? That we are at the point where I'm just glad they survived? That we are ready to be grateful for being allowed to live?

In my opinion, the mayor's office and the city council chambers should be packed every day with citizens demanding answers and demanding change. Elected officials who won't listen, or won't engage, should be challenged at the next election.

What usually happens instead is that we have a few days of social media screeching and everyone goes back to their lives. And we (black people) are a little more hesitant in our next interaction in the white world, a little more nervous, a little less free.

White people who use the police as their personal security force do so *because they can.* They can, because the police (as a system, not individual officers) play a vital role in suppressing POC, and always have. *Even when the officers are black themselves,* they enforce the dominant social construct—white supremacy. *(Aside: have you read Carter G. Woodson's take on education? Even 100 years later, he's spot on.)*

The police have to stop allowing themselves to be used as a tool in this vicious game—but it's complicated. They have to respond to calls. They have to assume they're in danger at any time. They have to make snap decisions. They have to recognize and resolve their own personal biases.

And then you have the officers who are eager and willing to engage in this blatantly racist behavior.

There is excellent and effective training for this, but cities have to be willing to consider it a priority (most don't) and be willing to spend the money. They'd rather buy bigger guns and riot gear.

The other consequence, of course, is financial. Montgomery fought the bus boycott because they were losing too much money without black riders. The governor of Arizona vetoed the anti-LGBTQ bill not out of belief in equality, but because the NFL, the MLB and others threatened to take their enterprises elsewhere. (Similar bills passed in Kentucky and other states with few tourists and *no financial consequences.)*

The black men in Philly settled for 200K, which is laughable. The City breathes a sigh of relief, writes a check, and changes nothing.

When people said in the 60s (as they do now) that laws don't change people's hearts, I think of this MLK quote: It may be true that the law cannot make a man love me, but it can keep him from lynching me and I think that is pretty important.

Their behavior will change when it starts costing them too much not to.

Question: I wonder if there might be less resistance [from whites]—and more possibility—if your [black people's] focus shifted from everything that was wrong to what is working? When I feel blamed, I shut down.

Answer: May I offer you some feedback? While I realize it wasn't intentional, your response is a perfect example of "white fragility": the idea that pointing out examples of racism and privilege in real time—as opposed to the abstract—is received as "shaming" and "blaming", and white participants choosing to affect the victim position.

Put another way: why should people of color—the actual victims of racism and oppression—be required to make your preferences the priority in these situations?

Ask yourself WHY you expect *even the dismantling of racism* to be done on your terms, with language you prefer, in ways where your comfort is centered?

Follow-up Question: I appreciate your tempered response. But, as long as we make it about us against them, won't the divisions persist?

Follow-up Answer: My response was not meant to be tempered at all—it was meant to prove a point. A point you demonstrated quite elegantly by thanking me for my nonconfrontational response— *because I surely value white praise, and so you encourage me to continue in this vein*—and then going on to say *it's still not enough.*

In the end, we're still not talking about racism, are we? No. *We're talking about how white people want to be addressed,* which becomes more important than the topic itself.

I lifted those words verbatim from the story: *May I offer you some feedback?* The point made, over and over, that no matter how polite or civil or conscious of white feelings we try to be, we get a version of this response: *Well if you would just center my white feelings of being comfortable instead of your black feelings of justifiable anger, if you would just talk more positively instead making me feel guilty, etc., well then maybe,* **maybe***, I'd hear you.*

And it's not even true. There are no words or magic approach that will make white people own their racism and start working to correct it—and we've been trying for 400+ years so we're the experts on what doesn't work. We will never meet your criteria for communicating in such a way that you will suddenly see the light—because you (generic you) don't want to own your racism, though you're perfectly happy to profit from it.

See what I just did? I put in "generic you" specifically so you don't have to take that comment personally. You can mentally excuse yourself. I centered your fragile white feelings instead of my black rage. Did it help?

May I offer you some feedback? I suggest you ask yourself a different question: How can you, as a white person of privilege, center the feelings of people of color who are telling you a truth you find uncomfortable? Can you, as a white person, remember that we are far more uncomfortable and in far more danger than you in any racial conversation or interaction? Can you, as a white person, stop swimming in your own feelings long enough to hear ours?

The bottom line is that all this advice for people of color about how best to communicate with white people proceeds from a time-worn false premise: that the responsibility for dismantling racism should fall on the victims, instead of where it actually belongs—on the perpetrators.

White people who truly want to understand and defeat racism can start by letting those most harmed by it lead the conversation—and processing their discomfort, guilt, indignation and whatever feelings come up—in healthy ways. Not by attempting to direct the tone and pitch of the discussion, or by insisting that people of color change the way we talk about it.

Or by pretending that *if we do change* the way we talk about, or the way we sound, or the way we act, you'll suddenly "understand" racism better.

Because we've been hearing that same old line for centuries.

Question: Why are people so easily offended? Being offended is a choice.

Answer: Maybe it is a choice—*for you.*

You're not at risk. You have the privilege of choosing what will or will not bother you.

For me, being offended is not a choice.

For me, being offended is an early warning system and a call to action. It alerts me that I'm in danger. That there are people nearby who wish me ill.

Being offended stiffens my spine so I can fight back. Maybe for my life.

The Klan's not burning crosses on *your* front lawn. I know, I know—you don't like the Klan. But they're not bothering *you*, are they?

You're not getting your head busted open for using the "wrong" bathroom, or for kissing your same-sex spouse in public.

ICE isn't coming to break down *your* door or rip *your* children out of your arms.

Anybody asking you for your passport at the grocery store?

You can lounge all day in Starbucks and, miraculously, no police will be called. You can stand in your grandmother's backyard, day or night, no shots fired.

You're safe. I'm not. *Millions of us are not safe.*

When you say "I love everybody. Even gays," you reveal the problem.

Listen—there will be no love—and no peace—until there is justice. Until there is equal treatment under the law. Until there is freedom from fear.

Until that day, all your talk of "love" is about as useful as throwing a shiny tarp over a pile of broken bodies, climbing on top, and singing Kumbaya.

Completely worthless.

Chapter 14

Risky Business: What High-Risk Kids Teach Us About Communicating

Originally published June 4, 2018 in Creative Conduct on Medium.com

On my first day of work at the community center, I wasn't nervous. After all, I'd supervised youth "delinquents" in corrections programs; I'd worked juvenile probation. I knew this gang-run neighborhood was teeming with kids who had few choices, and even fewer resources. I knew exactly what they needed: structure, guidance, mentoring. To say no to drugs and yes to education.

I expected to put in 2–3 years and move up and out.

I was not expecting Marco.

Marco was not impressed with me or my college education. He was living a life I could barely comprehend: he'd been stabbed, beaten, set on fire and burned (on purpose) with an iron. In the first year I worked there, he was shot at, hit by a car and "violated" by his gang—meaning they'd taken turns beating him with their fists over some rule infraction.

He lived in abandoned buildings, shoplifted daily and once wrapped his 6-year-old cousin's head in duct tape to make him stop crying. He slept on the back seat of cars while his mother gave blow jobs in the front. He carried drugs for his uncles, guns for his gang, and money for dealers.

He was 13.

Over the next several years, Marco and his friends taught me fact from fiction and reality from textbook about high-risk kids. Because I didn't go after 3 years, or 10 years, or 25.

I simply couldn't leave them.

Here's what I learned:

If you've spent any time with children, you know that they are the world's best lie detectors. They seem to intuitively know when the adults around them are sincere.

For kids living in high-risk environments, this is doubly true. These kids have learned to read body language and voice tones like FBI profilers. For some, it's a matter of survival. They have developed the ability to "hear" when the adults around them are escalating from argument to violence; to "see" a looming problem like an eviction; and to "feel" the tension that means "it's time to run".

In this risky world, disobeying adults is often warranted, and only occasionally punished. These kids will generally act on their own instincts, rather than your directions. They will trust their own feelings in any given situation, rather than your guidelines.

Of course, they have neither the maturity nor the life experience to realize that this approach is badly flawed.

This reliance on their own judgment has kept them safe many times. It becomes reflexive, even in situations where it's clearly detrimental.

In a classroom, this will look like defiance, disrespect or disobedience.

There are a few ways to combat this:

Be Authentic

Create an environment in which it is "safe" for them to follow directions without question. A space where the rules are clear, fair and consistent; where corrections are given with love and respect; and where their compliance does not come with humiliation.

Practice being non-competitive in interactions. Project calm, loving, assertive energy. If you have hidden doubts about your own authority, they'll know.

Remember that your tone of voice and your facial expressions will have more impact than your actual words, at least at the outset. You probably know someone who says the nicest words with the coldest intent. Or, as Marco called it, "the shine".

Be willing to build relationships with them. They are accustomed to superficiality and manipulation. Authenticity will be met first with confusion, and then with joy.

Listen

If you listen to kids, especially if they're younger than 14 or so, they'll tell you everything you need to know.

If you don't know what their lives are like, then you're not paying attention.

Are they verbally abusive or sarcastic or fond of name-calling? This is how people talk to them. Are they quick to take offense? Easily insulted? Slow to apologize? This accurately reflects the adults in their lives. Do they hit first and ask questions later? They are accustomed to being hit first, with explanations coming later, if at all.

Do they routinely mischaracterize or misunderstand the statements of others? Remember that we need language even to think. Poor language skills will directly impact their ability to think clearly and communicate effectively.

They need words to identify emotions, concepts, ideas—words they often don't have. Boys, especially, may not even be able to identify any emotions other than rage or sexual arousal. Fear, sadness, loneliness, anxiety, etc., may all be interpreted as anger.

Listen to your kids. Listen to their conversations, their weekend adventures, their favorite music. Give them the words they need to think critically. Help them build a vocabulary that includes optimism, hope, determination and self-worth.

Know the Difference Between Discipline and Punishment

You are administering effective discipline when:

1. The child's safety and well-being is your primary goal.

2. Your boundaries are clear, fair and understood.

3. Your boundaries do not change based on your emotions.

4. Your boundaries are enforced consistently and impartially.

5. You are feeling calm; you have no internal doubts about what you're requiring.

You are administering punishment when:

The assertion of your authority (and the child's submission to that authority) is your primary goal.

2. Your boundaries sometimes inadvertently result in favoritism.

3. Your boundaries change based on your energy level or your feelings.

Your boundaries have been breached without comment in the past, leading to an overcorrection.

You are feeling angry, self-righteous or resentful.

Be the Change You Want to See

Kids in high-risk environments develop a set of destructive behaviors and attitudes which have long-term effects on school performance, social acceptance and economic success. You cannot argue, punish or reason them out of these attitudes.

But you can provide them with an alternate world view.

You can model peaceful conflict resolution.

You can give them opportunities to achieve their goals.

Here is what Marco said when he aged out of program:

I felt like I was in a box. I couldn't get out, and my counselor couldn't get in. He tried to help me, but there was no way in or out. He could see the door, but I couldn't. Then I got arrested with my boys. For the first time, I realized I had choices. For the first time, I thought hey maybe there really IS a way to get out. I did my 6 months in jail and came back to program. I didn't trust anybody, at first. But I trusted my counselor. He said there was a way, and he had never lied to me, so I kept looking until I found it.

Unlike so many of his contemporaries, Marco found the door.

You can BE the change.

Chapter 15

Are You Ready? Because Here It Is

Originally published November 20, 2017 on Medium.com

He was a 70-year-old Catholic priest, which was an odd sort of friend for me to have. Of course, he was an odd sort of priest, and as I've noted often, weird people dig me. The bishop called him Trouble, because he had no respect for authority; the parishioners called him Crazy, but not in a bad way; and I called him whenever I was in trouble, which was twice a week.

I was running a gang-diversion program from a community center, and he operated a soup kitchen right around the corner. We were natural allies in the war on poverty, and as we discovered one night after a spate of neighborhood shootings, well-suited drinking buddies.

Two teenagers—two of my boys—dead in less than a week. Two more speeding away in an ambulance, while I paced in front of the rectory, sick and scared and barely able to breathe.

"You have to go to the hospital," he said, using his Altar Voice— The One You Dared Not Disobey. "These boys have no one but you."

"But I'm not ready for this," I whispered. Not ready to see them arrested and jailed. Not ready to see them bloody and broken. Not ready to watch them die.

He shook his head. "Well, you must be ready," he said. "Because here it is in your path."

I was in no mood for mystical metaphors. "What?"

"Nothing appears in your life until you are ready for it. If it's here—you must be ready."

Sounded like another God Moves in Mysterious Ways lecture coming on, and I snapped.

"Oh, spare me that bullshit," I shot back. "Were these boys "ready" to be shot? Were the children watching "ready" to see this violence?

And then, unforgivably, I said, "Were you "ready" for your wife to die of cancer?"

I tried to suck the words back into my mouth. But I had no time to apologize or regroup.

He was beaming at me. A big, booming, loving smile. And then laughing out loud.

"You're confusing "want to" with "ready to". You may not want to feel this pain or witness what is bound to be an agonizing sequence of events. But you are ready to do it." His eyes twinkled. "That's the definition of ready: Here. It. Is."

He hugged me, still grinning like a nut. "You need a ride to the hospital?"

Father Ray—a tall, skinny guy who somehow managed to look like Santa Claus—was a rebel by nature. In the 1960's, he'd been marching for better wages with the migrant farm workers when he met a passionate young widow on the picket line. He fell in love and left the priesthood to marry a black woman and raise 8 children. He nursed her during the last years of her life, and when she passed, he came back to the priesthood, to our peculiar little parish.

Our church—multi-racial, multi-lingual, and in the heart of a struggling neighborhood—welcomed him and his posse of biracial grandchildren. He wore African kente cloth robes while saying the Mass, and never took off his wedding ring. He embraced black Catholic traditions, gospel music, and old-fashioned revivals.

He was a social justice warrior, and he advocated tirelessly for the poor. His years with the farmers, too, had left their mark, and he'd lapse into Spanish without thinking. He dug up all the grass behind the church and planted vegetables.

He gave me lots of poetic, if unwanted, advice over the years.

During a lengthy criminal trial, when it seemed there would be no justice:

If there is a mountain looming up before you—look behind that tree for your mountain climbing gear.

When the number of gang-involved kids at the center far exceeded our capacity, but I couldn't turn anyone away:

If a raging river sweeps across your path—your inflatable raft is somewhere nearby.

After a funding crisis, with no solution in sight:

If a pit suddenly gapes open at your feet—take off your shirt so your wings can unfurl.

And always, no matter what the crisis was:

I promise you—if He left an obstacle in your way, He also left you everything you need to overcome it.

I still don't go to Mass, and when people throw Bible verses in my face I'm liable to roll my eyes (or worse). But Fr. Ray didn't discard me for that; he just helped me see the connections in my own unorthodox ways.

And no matter what shows up in my life today, tomorrow or next week—I know it means I must be ready for it.

Chapter 16

The Power of Failure

Originally published June 15, 2018 in the Startup on Medium.com

If We Want to Empower Girls, We Have to Let Them Fail

After a week of cool but unusually sunny weather in southern Scotland, I arrived in Fort William, ready to hike Ben Nevis. I needed to get my first lungful of Highland air, and stock supplies for the next 7 days on the Great Glen Way.

The rain hit first thing in the morning. A sprinkle at first, then sheets of icy drizzle, then a downpour. This did not surprise me. It is Scotland, after all. I had rain gear and waterproof hiking boots and a good supply of single-malt.

What did surprise me was the number of parents with kids out on what was now a treacherously slick path, headed uphill. One family was picking its way up the rocky slope just ahead of me.

The girl, who looked to be about 10 or 11, was constantly bombarded with advice, directions and cautionary commentary.

"Watch out!" they yelled at her. "Be careful!" "Don't hurt yourself!" And my personal favorite: "You're getting mud in your hair!"

The boy, who was younger and smaller, received far different guidance:

"Did you fall? You're all right. Get up, keep moving."

"Wow, isn't that mountain big? Look at that!"

"Tighten your boot laces. Adjust your poles. The rocks are slippery."

We made the crest at roughly the same time, all of us cold, wet, muddy and miserable. (I was perhaps not as miserable as the rest. I had the scotch, after all.)

The little girl was asked again and again if she'd been scared, and told how brave she was, and reminded to fix her hair.

The boy got a high-five and a "That was pretty cool, huh?"

(Full disclosure: all my righteous indignation for this little girl evaporated when she turned to me and asked, "How old are you anyway?" But that's not the point.)

The point is that, all too often, this is how boys and girls learn about their capabilities.

Boys learn to make their decisions in spite of fear.

Girls learn to let fear make their decisions.

Boys learn to keep trying, to endure pain or discomfort, to stand their ground.

Girls learn to hesitate, to react to the smallest discomfort, to stand and wait.

Upon my return from Scotland, I gave a talk about women hiking solo to a group of professional managers.

The men in the room asked:

How did you train for that?

What amazing things did you see and do?

What was it like? Are you glad you went?

Where are you going next?

Women wanted to know:

How did you get off work?

What did you do about your kids/elderly parents/pets?

How much did it cost?

Weren't you afraid?

Have I been afraid, lost in the woods with darkness coming on?

Have I been afraid, realizing I'm on the wrong bus to the wrong city?

Have I been afraid, alone and unable to speak the native language?

Of course, I have.

Would I trade feeling safe for feeling accomplished?

Not a chance.

The only antidote to fear is action.

We teach that to our boys, relentlessly. Why not our girls?

If you want girls to succeed, you have to let them fail. Let them get cold and hungry. Let them discover the right trail after 3 false turns.

Let them see that magnificent view from the top of the mountain. Let them figure out the bus schedule in a foreign city. Let them live on cheese and apples and cold showers for a few days. Let them strike up conversations with interesting strangers.

Let them discover for themselves how capable they are.

Let some little girl in the future watch them hike up a mountain, and ask, "Just how old are you, anyway?"

We have fallen into the destructive habit of worrying more about "making kids feel good about themselves" instead of giving them opportunities to work toward a goal. The solution to this muddle is actually simple: If you want self-esteem, then do estimable things. Accomplishments and know-how can't be handed out. They must be earned through individual effort.

~Psychology Today

Chapter 17

My Faith in Broccoli

In 2015, I left my community center and urban farm for 3 weeks to walk the Camino Portuguese, a 150-mile trek up the rocky coast of Portugal and through the Spanish countryside. The farmers I met didn't speak to me of seeds or sun or chemical enhancements. They only spoke of faith.

While the collard greens grew in the most unlikely places in Portugal—seaside gardens and hilly backyards—the Spanish farms wound their way around vineyards and valleys, up rocky crests and through flocks of chickens. In Portugal, the old people would walk up and hand me food: fresh baked bread, cheese, raw scallops fresh from the sea. In Spain, the gifts were left for me—lush, purple grapes arranged like still-life art on the stone borders of crumbling old churches.

The farmers called their greens the Galician word for "cabbage" but they were actually collard greens. Collard greens unlike any I'd ever seen before—they grew on tall stalks, with the leaves starting about half way up, making them very easy to weed, water and harvest. My greens at home grew in marked contrast, looking more like wild bushes. Weeding the collard beds was backbreaking work.

How did they get them to grow so tall and straight in Spain?

At last, a farmer stood near the road with his teenaged daughter. The old man nodded at my backpack and pilgrim's shell, murmured *"Buen Camino"*. His hand outstretched, he offered me a chunk of bread from his pocket, and a small, perfect apple. I clutched them to my chest. This was my 9th or 10th day on the Camino; I'd learned not to offer money in return.

"Please," I said to the girl. "How do you make them grow like this?" I pulled out my phone and showed them pics of my greens, growing like wild bushes in the dirt back in Illinois. The old man looked at my phone and back a half-dozen times before it clicked and his cautious smile morphed into a full-fledged grin.

"To make yours grow like this, you have to give some to the poor. And St. James will bless your crops." The old man spread his arms out, sweeping in the vista of his well-kept farm. *"Las bendiciones de Santiago,"* he said. The blessings of St. James.

I certainly saw some parallels in my center's garden back home. We were clearly blessed beyond measure.

Maybe it WAS because we gave away most of what we grew. What else could explain the continual growth and expansion of our garden when we had no idea what we were doing? When we planted the lettuces in full sun and the broccoli in the shade and the tomatoes under a tree, and yet they all flourished?

The onion sets were upside down, but they grew hard and fast and turned themselves up to the sun. We had crazy green ones growing in pretzel shapes—but growing, nonetheless.

We had one bed where the broccoli had spread out under the cherry tomatoes, so much so that we couldn't even get the tomato cages in the ground without bruising the broccoli, so we let them grow together, wild and untamed. Harvesting them was like going on safari—I had to get down on my knees, stick my head into the thick foliage, and scavenge.

A visitor watching me do this one day asked a simple question: Why didn't we prune them back? Or just pull up the broccoli?

Oh, if we pull it up it'll probably die, I remember telling him. We haven't had much luck transplanting broccoli.

He shrugged. So, what? "You've got plenty of broccoli," he said, nodding to the other beds. "You don't need this one."

I did, indeed, have a lot of broccoli. The kids loved it. "Well," I knew this would sound ridiculous, but I pressed on. "The kids will wonder what happened to it, you know? They'll ask me where I put it, and if it's all right, and why can't they see it." I shrugged.

Truth be told, it hurt me, too, when I had to sacrifice a plant, or when I lost one from my own ignorance. This plant, this broccoli that was planted in too-acidic soil, too much shade, and getting too little water—this broccoli plant was growing full and strong, and I had no intention of getting in its way.

Just like the neighborhood kids. They didn't get enough of anything they needed—food, education, clothes, role models. Some of them didn't even get much parenting. They were planted in a hostile environment, surrounded by violence and drugs and poor examples.

But they were growing, just the same. They were pushing through the contaminated soil, fighting off the invaders, reaching for the sun, no matter what.

We weren't going to discard them either. We were going to make as much space for them as we could in the bad soil and the lousy water and the bed with too many pests. We were going to pull the weeds that were choking them and help them live to fight another day. And at harvest, we were going to get in there with both hands and save all the fruit we could reach.

From the dirt, I remember looking up at my visitor, who didn't think I needed this untamed broccoli plant. I'm sure my face was scratched and my hat was askew and my t-shirt was riding up over my waistband. "Yes, I do," I said. "I need this one, too." I gave him a brilliant smile that he didn't understand.

In Spain, I watched the farmer and his daughter turn toward a patch of what looked to be squash leaves and drop to their knees.

They would've understood about my broccoli.

They would've understood completely.

Chapter 18

Happy Birthday, America

Originally published July 4, 2018 on Medium.com

Every 4th of July, National Public Radio (NPR) broadcasts a dramatic reading of the Declaration of Independence. Last year, the organization tweeted the document, line by line, phrase by phrase, and encouraged Americans to read it aloud in order to re-create its powerful message.

Who can fail to be moved by these words?

We hold these truths to be self-evident, that all men are created equal, that they are endowed by their Creator with certain unalienable rights, that among these are Life, Liberty and the Pursuit of Happiness.

But the Declaration was not just eloquent prose; it was revolution. Asserting that we the people have not just the right to alter or abolish a destructive government, but a duty to do so. The Founding Fathers, of course, were speaking of King George of England.

But by 2017, unfortunately, the cracks in our democracy—and the sheer ignorance of far too many Americans—was already beginning to show. As NPR tweeted the Declaration, replies flooded in, accusing the nonpartisan media group of "propaganda" and "inciting violence and revolution", of stirring insurrection against the Trump White House.

At least one Trump supporter opined that the Declaration of Independence was "fake news trash".

Once the error was pointed out, many tweeters deleted their remarks, no doubt from embarrassment. It was a chilling reminder of how easy it is to forget our history— and then attack those who point out the truth.

We can't detach ourselves from the past and expect to build a future.

In 1776, some of us were far more "equal" than others, an injustice still not fully rectified today. As abolitionist and ex-slave Frederick Douglass said in his famous July 4, 1852 speech, the "scorching irony" of black men celebrating America's liberty was not lost on him:

"What, to the American slave, is your 4th of July? I answer; a day that reveals to him, more than all other days in the year, the gross injustice and cruelty to which he is the constant victim. To him, your celebration is a sham; your boasted liberty, an unholy license; your national greatness, swelling vanity; your sound of rejoicing are empty and heartless; your denunciation of tyrants brass fronted impudence; your shout of liberty and equality, hollow mockery; your prayers and hymns, your sermons and thanksgivings, with all your religious parade and solemnity, are to him, mere bombast, fraud, deception, impiety, and hypocrisy—a thin veil to cover up crimes which would disgrace a nation of savages. There is not a nation on the earth guilty of practices more shocking and bloody than are the people of the United States, at this very hour."

Some 158 years later, President Barack Obama would call the launch of those 13 rebellious colonies an "improbable experiment in democracy" which still lives and breathes some 242 years later. The Declaration never once acknowledges the lives of women or black slaves (although the "merciless Indian savages" rate a mention).

Yet our commitment to this document and its ideals have, time and time again, advanced the cause of human rights here and around the world.

It reminds us—as NPR will again today—that we have not just the right, but the obligation, to resist oppression, whatever its source. That our nation was born out of dissension and protest and grew into a world power because we refuse to submit to tyrants. And that despite all its flaws, democracy is the last, best hope for our planet.

So, as you celebrate America's birthday today, remember the unwavering idealism of the Founders—and the bitter rage of Frederick Douglass. Remember that both called for decisive action, resistance and resolve in the face of oppression.

Remember that freedom is not free, and there is a price to be paid to defend our Constitution from all enemies, foreign and domestic.

Remember that whether your forbears were natives to this land, or whether they arrived on a ship—willingly or in chains—we are all in the same boat now.

And this boat we're in—sea-worthy and time-tested though it may be—is heading for a storm the likes of which we've never seen in our lifetimes.

I hope we're ready.

Happy Birthday, America.

About Warren-Sharpe Community Center

At Warren-Sharpe, we are planting the seeds of change.

The Center has provided social services on Joliet, Illinois' south and east sides since 1991, including: gang intervention, parenting classes, after-school programs, summer camp, food pantry, and nutrition education. Our garden--Green Sprout Urban Farm--has grown into several lots that feed children in our summer and after-school programs, 600 unduplicated households through our food pantry, and other members of the community.

Warren-Sharpe is committed to addressing the root causes of poverty, to dismantling racism in the food system, and to economic self-sufficiency for the families in our community. We know we can rebuild our community.

Warren-Sharpe is a 501(c)(3) charity. All proceeds from this book support food programs and youth empowerment projects at the Center.

Visit us online at https://www.Warren-SharpeCommunityCenter.org or on Facebook.

About the Author

Kay Bolden is a writer, speaker, community organizer, backpacker and tree hugger. She grew up during the turbulent 1960's, the daughter of civil rights activists. For 25 years, she directed the Warren-Sharpe Community Center and its social enterprise, Green Sprout Urban Farm, in Joliet, Illinois. The Center works to eradicate social inequalities, to build an equitable food system, and to empower youth and families of color.

She has published numerous articles on community development, women's empowerment and personal growth, and she blogs regularly at KayBolden.com and on Medium.com. She saves her political rants for Twitter.

Kay lives in San Diego, California where she is working on her second novel, and still searching for the perfect microbrew.

9 781722 361235